A 3-minute forever book

EAT
YOUR
PEAS™

for Girlfriends

written by Cheryl Karpen
illustrated by Sandy Fougner

Gently Spoken Communications

Friends
do not live in harmony merely,
as some say,
but in melody.

Henry David Thoreau

November 13, 2005

To Shellie

in celebration of our

friendship

with love from Sharon

At the
heart of this little book
is a *promise*.
It's a promise from me
to you
and it goes like this:

Whenever
you'd like a friend to
laugh with, cry with, vent to,
brag to or celebrate with...

call me.

I promise
to be the one who
listens
with all my heart
and without interrupting.
(yes, really !)

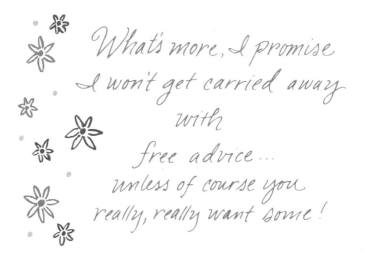

What's more, I promise
I won't get carried away
with
free advice...
unless of course you
really, really want some!

In the meantime...
here's what I want you to

know,

remember,

take to heart,

memorize

and

never, ever doubt.

Have I told you
lately how
important
you are to me...

how much *better* my life is
because *you* are in it?

You are
kind,
compassionate,
lovely,
courageous,
intelligent,
fun
and a
precious and spirited
friend.

I cherish you.

All the stars in the universe

danced

on the day you were born.

Imagine

There is not another you
in the whole world.

There is not another me.

We met and we became friends.

Imagine
that!

When I think
of you
I
smile.

Sometimes I miss
our time alone together,
don't you?

· creating · listening · crying · dining ·

A TIME JUST-FOR-US

CERTIFICATE

Anytime.
Anyplace.
(your choice!)

value: priceless

dancing · relaxing

gardening · laughing · walking · playing ·

crafting · talking

One of my favorite things
about being around you is...

I get to be myself!

Wouldn't it be fun to be

Queen
for a
Day?

If you bring the tea, I'll bring the crowns!

Don't you dare
clean
the house
before I come over!

I love you just the way you are.
Unconditionally.

I never, ever want to hurt you.

So if I ever say anything that
hurts your feelings,
please, please ask me about it because
it will make me aware,
or give me the opportunity to explain
and above all,
it will give me a chance to say
I'm sorry.

Sometimes when we're together
and it seems like we've used up
all our words,

just knowing you're near
warms my heart.

I
love how you always
seem to

understand me.

Let's plan a night in (or away!) with our nearest and dearest friends,

a really late night (past 8:00 pm!) with pillows and pj's (holes and all!).

We'll tell stories.

Laugh.

Celebrate friendships.

Relax, rejuvenate and renew.

(Makes me smile just thinking about it!)

Imagine how boring
our friendship
would be if we agreed on
e v e r y t h i n g.

Instead, let's agree to
celebrate
our differences.

It's true!
One can never have enough:

____ blooming things
____ **comfy shoes**
____ page turners
____ **yummy lingerie**

Let's go shopping!

If you are ever tempted
to run away
(and who isn't!)

think about how much
I'd miss you!

Everyday
take some time to
fill your spirit
with things you
love to do.

Your whole-hearted joy
depends on it.

It's tough being
everything to everybody.

Why not cut yourself some slack?

Let's do something
just for you.

Gratitude

is a **gift you give yourself**.

So give thanks for
all the wonders that touch your days.

Fresh water.
Clean sheets.
A nap in the sun.
Spirited friends.
A bra that fits.
And what would the world
be without chocolate!

Dream. Dream. Dream.

Hold on to your
dreams
dear friend.

Anything is possible.

Believe
in
yourself.

I do.

I believe
You are a very important Somebody.

It doesn't matter if you just won the lottery or if you have to count every penny.

It doesn't matter if you have it all together or if you can never find your car keys.

It doesn't matter where you work (or don't) or what anyone else you know has accomplished (or not).

You are a very important Somebody
and

I am so glad you are my friend.

Thank you for all the times
you've listened without judgement,

for gently **lifting my spirit** with
gifts of perspective...

for reminding me
that things really do get better.

(But then, how could it be otherwise
with you as my friend?)

Whether you are near or far,
I will always hold
our friendship
close to
my
heart.

Cherish each day.
(indulge yourself)

Play whenever you can
(celebrate yourself)

and most of all...

take good care of yourself.

Remember to always...

eat your peas!

Why Peas?

She was a vibrant, dazzling young woman with a promising future.
Yet, at sixteen, her world felt sad and hopeless.

I was living over 1800 miles away and wanted to let this very special young person in my life know I would be there for her across the miles and through the darkness. I wanted her to know she could call me any time, at any hour, and I would be there for her. And I wanted to give her a piece of my heart she could take with her anywhere—a reminder she was loved.

Really loved.

Her name is Maddy and she was the inspiration for my first PEAS book, Eat Your Peas™ for Young Adults. At the very beginning of her book I made a place to write in my phone number so she knew I was serious about being available. And right beside the phone number I put my promise to listen—really listen—whenever that call came.

Soon after the book was published, people began to ask me if I had the same promise and affirmation for adults. I realized it isn't just young people who need to be reminded how truly special they are. **We all do.**

Today Maddy is thriving and giving hope to others in her life.
If someone has given you this book it means **you are a pretty amazing person** to them and they wanted to let you know. Take it to heart.

Believe it, and remind yourself often.

Wishing you peas and plenty of joy,

 **Cheryl Karpen**

P.S. If you are wondering why I named the collection, Eat Your Peas...it's my way of saying, "Stay healthy. I love and cherish you. I want you to live **forever!**"

With gratitude...

Every time I begin growing a new idea, I am humbled by the
knowledge that I am only one of the peas in the pod.
I only plant the seed, help nurture it and watch it grow.
Amazing people help turn my garden of dreams into a reality.

When **Sandy Fougner**, the illustrator of Eat Your Peas™ Collection,
began weaving her artistry into my gift shops and my books,
I didn't realize I would receive the greatest gift of all —
her gentle and honest friendship. Thank you, Sandy, for your passion
for Peas and for sharing your gift with girlfriends everywhere.
You are all heart and it shows.

My editor, **Suzanne Foust**, always makes me sound better than I really am.
You are a blessing to me, Suzanne.

Lana Siewert-Olson is the the newest Pea in our Pod. Lana is a saint.
She is our printer.

A special thank you to my sister **Jeanne Grams**,
my dear friend **Mary Lund** and to all my girlfriends
who allow me to share in their lives.

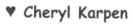

♥ Cheryl Karpen

Other books by Cheryl Karpen

The Eat Your Peas™ Collection

Takes only 3-minutes to read
but you'll want to hold on to them forever!

Eat Your Peas for Sisters
Eat Your Peas for Daughters
Eat Your Peas for Sons
Eat Your Peas for Mothers
Eat Your Peas for New Moms
Eat Your Peas for Grandkids
Eat Your Peas for Young Adults
Eat Your Peas for Gardening Friends

New titles are SPROUTING up all the time!

Heart and Soul Collection

To Let You Know I Care
Hope for a Hurting Heart
Can We Try Again? Finding a way to love

To view a complete collection, visit us on-line at **eatyourpeas.com**

Eat Your Peas™ for Girlfriends

Copyright 2001, Cheryl Karpen

For more information or to locate a store near you contact:

Gently Spoken Communications
P.O. Box 245
Anoka, Minnesota 55303
1-877-224-7886
www.eatyourpeas.com

A portion of the profits from the
Eat your Peas Collection™
will benefit empowerment programs
for youth and adults.